CAREGIVER'S WORKBOOK

Denise Hoover

Midlife Choices LLC

ISBN 979-8-218-84759-3

Have You Read *Surviving My Husband's Stroke* Yet?

This workbook is a companion to my memoir, *Surviving My Husband's Stroke*. If you haven't read it yet, I encourage you to check it out. In it, I share the raw, honest story of becoming my husband's caregiver after his stroke, and what it truly takes to find your way forward.

Get your copy of *Surviving My Husband's Stroke* — available in paperback and ebook wherever books are sold.

Table of CONTENTS

Introduction

Post-stroke caregiving is overwhelming, frustrating, and emotional. Overnight, you become the one holding everything together at home while trying to figure out how to support your husband through recovery.

The days quickly fill with doctor visits, therapy sessions, medication schedules, paperwork, and never-ending chores. On top of that, you're also trying to squeeze in recovery activities while trying to find time to do the laundry or the bills.

It's exhausting. **Some days you wonder how you'll survive it all.**

I created this workbook because I've been exactly where you are. When my husband, Jeff, had his stroke, I suddenly became not only his caregiver but also the manager of our entire life. I was drained, scattered, and holding it all together with piles of file folders, notebooks, and sticky notes covering my kitchen table. My "system" was really no system at all—it only added to the overwhelm.

I knew there had to be a better way. That's why I created this workbook. It's designed to keep everything in one place—appointments, medications, recovery notes—so you don't feel like you're drowning in scraps of paper and endless to-do lists.

But this isn't just about staying organized. This workbook also gives you space to sort through your emotions, reflect on your experiences, and take care of yourself along the way.

Looking back, I wish I'd had something like this to help me feel a little more in control.

I know how chaotic and lonely caregiving can feel, and my hope is that this workbook becomes your comforting place to come back to for organization, coping, and emotional release.

To help with that, the workbook is divided into sections. Each one is designed with a purpose: from planning daily tasks and managing medical information, to coping with emotions and remembering meaningful moments. Here's what you'll find inside:

Section One: Strategies for Coping
In this section, you'll find guidance and exercises to help you work through the emotional side of caregiving. Each part is structured with instruction, a guided activity, and space for reflection so you can process your feelings and find practical ways to cope.

Introduction

Section Two: Planning

This section helps you keep track of the endless details—appointments, medications, essential information, and future plans. It's about getting everything out of your head and onto paper so you can stay organized without the overwhelm.

Section Three: Surviving

In this section, you'll find tools to capture meaningful moments, explore your emotions through journaling, and reframe your role as a caregiver. It's about survival in the truest sense—finding ways to keep going without losing who you are.

Bonus Section: Aphasia Exercises

If your husband struggles with aphasia, this bonus section offers simple, practical activities I used with my husband. These tools are designed to help with relearning words, objects, and communication in everyday life.

When I first stepped into this role, I often felt like I was barely keeping my head above water. The responsibilities, the emotions, the constant unknowns—it all added up so quickly. I don't want you to feel that same sense of drowning. My hope is that this workbook becomes a steady companion for you—a place to unload, organize, and reflect. Use it however it helps you most, whether that's keeping track of appointments or simply getting your feelings down on paper.

This isn't about doing everything perfectly—it's about giving yourself space to breathe and reminding yourself that you're doing the best you can. You are not alone in this journey, and I hope these pages bring both comfort and clarity when you need them most.

And if you ever need extra pages along the way, you'll find free printable downloads waiting for you at www.denisehoover.com/workbook.

Courage doesn't always roar. Sometimes courage is the quiet voice at the end of the day saying, "I will try again tomorrow."

-Mary Anne Radmacher

Strategies for Coping

*When emotions run high, these small acts can help
you pause, reset, and move forward.*

Strategies for Coping

Coping doesn't mean you're fine—it means you're doing what you can to keep it together when everything around you feels like it's falling apart. It's not about fixing anything. You're not broken—you're just trying to make it through the hard parts.

I snapped at my husband more times than I care to admit. I didn't want to be mean to him, but there were days when frustration and exhaustion got the best of me. And every time I lost my temper, it felt like I was scolding a child for bothering me. That's not how I wanted to treat my husband.

Over time, I had to develop coping strategies to keep myself from reaching that snapping point. These small acts gave me a moment to pause—a chance to create some space between his needs and my frustration.

As his recovery continued, I realized I was unintentionally adding to the stress of the situation—mostly through the way I was thinking and reacting. I wasn't treating my husband like the partner I married. I was treating him like a nuisance. I snapped at the smallest things he said or did, until I reminded myself: This is an adult man who has survived a brain injury. He wasn't fully aware of the changes in his personality. He didn't realize his emotional reactions weren't typical.

I had to figure out how to change my behavior—so that I could feel less overwhelmed, and so he didn't feel like a burden in everyday moments.

What helped were small strategies. Things I could do in the moment to ease my anxiety, reduce the tension, and treat my husband the way he deserved to be treated.

That's what this section is all about.

Each strategy starts with a short explanation, followed by a guided activity, and ends with space to reflect on what worked—or didn't. You can write, skip, come back, or do the same page five times. And please, be honest. **Even if what you write feels too raw or a little nasty—this workbook is for your eyes only.**

If you try one small act and it helps, that's a win. If it doesn't, that's okay too. **You're still showing up. And that's the bravest thing of all.**

These are the things that helped me take a breath instead of snapping, step away instead of shutting down, and survive the hardest days. Some will feel right for you, some won't. Try them, test them, and trust yourself.

How to Develop Patience

INSTRUCTION

Choose one of the small acts below that helps you catch your breath or feel like yourself again. That's the one you'll start using the next time you feel like you're about to snap.

The key is to notice the anger before it boils over. Pay attention to how it feels in your body —tight jaw, fast heart, shallow breath—and **go with your intuition**.

BREATHE	WALK	CHANGE	LOOK AWAY
Take a deep breath. Let it out, slowly.	Walk away. Count to ten, silently.	Change the subject. Choose a generic topic.	Turn your head. Count to three, silently.

MANTRA	REPEAT	RESET	CLOSE EYES
Put your hand on your chest. Say, "This is hard, but I am strong."	Repeat a phrase like: "I'm grateful he's alive."	Excuse yourself. Go and splash cold water on your face.	Close your eyes. Remember, this is your husband.

Notice when your chosen act works—and when it doesn't.

Some moments will be easier than others. If your first strategy doesn't help in a certain situation, try a different one next time. The more you practice, the more you'll start to recognize which coping act fits which moment.

You're not failing—you're learning. Be gentle with yourself.

How to Develop Patience

Think about a moment when you felt close to snapping at your husband. Which small act of patience did you use—and how did it go?

Date

Small Act of Patience Used:

Describe how it worked:

What you would do differently:

How to Develop Patience

Date

Small Act of Patience Used:

Describe how it worked:

What you would do differently:

Patience takes practice. If you lose your temper, don't beat yourself up—you're human. This recovery period is hard on both of you. It takes time to figure out what helps, so be kind to yourself and keep using what works.

How to Develop Patience

This isn't just about staying calm in the moment. It's about creating a home where both of you can recover without fear, tension, or shame.

More patience might mean fewer arguments, gentler conversations, or even moments of quiet connection that help you both heal.

How has patience changed the way you respond to your husband?

Have patience. All things are difficult before they become easy.

-Saadi Shirazi

Need more *Developing Patience* pages?
Download free extras at: www.denisehoover.com/workbook

Managing Caregiver Guilt

Guilt is sneaky. It tells you that you're not doing enough, even when you're running on empty.

Guilt usually shows up in the form of *"Should"* statements:
I should be more patient. I shouldn't need a break. I should be able to handle this better.

But *"should"* doesn't mean true. Most of the time, it just means pressured.

This exercise helps you notice guilt-filled thoughts—and gently reframe them with compassion.

I should be able to handle this better.

Is this true?   No. I've never been in this situation before.

What can you say instead with compassion?   You're doing the best you can for your husband.

I shouldn't feel resentment.

Is this true?   No. I'm human.

What can you say instead with compassion?   It's ok to feel both love and frustration.

You may never completely get rid of guilt—but you can start to see it for what it is: a signal, not a truth. It's your mind's way of signaling you to slow down and pay attention.

"Should" statements don't help. When guilt creeps in, pause and ask yourself: Who says I should? Is this guilt trying to tell me something useful—or just making me feel worse?

Managing Caregiver Guilt

GUIDED ACTIVITY

Write down a few of the *"should"* or *"shouldn't"* thoughts that make you feel guilty. Then, underneath each one, challenge it.

Date

I should/shouldn't

Is this true? Explain:

What can you say instead with compassion?

Managing Caregiver Guilt

Date

I should/shouldn't

Is this true? Explain:

What can you say instead with compassion?

Guilt has a way of showing up even when you've done nothing wrong—especially when you're caring for your husband. It often comes from being overwhelmed, exhausted, or expecting too much of yourself. Instead of letting those thoughts take over, try to reframe them. **Guilt isn't proof that you've failed—it's a sign you care deeply and are doing your best in a hard situation.**

Managing Caregiver Guilt

REFLECTION

What would you say to a friend in your shoes-someone who feels guilty and is being hard on herself?

Would you expect her to be perfect? Would you tell her she's failing, or would you remind her that she's doing the best she can under impossible circumstances?

Take a moment to speak to yourself the way you'd speak to her.

Date

Guilt is always hungry; don't let it consume you.
— *Terri Guillemets*

Need more *Caregiver Guilt* pages?
Download free extras at: www.denisehoover.com/workbook

13

Redefining Normal

INSTRUCTION

Life may never go back to the way it was before your husband's stroke—and admitting that is one of the hardest parts. It hurts to let go of the familiar.

But just because the old version of *"normal"* is gone doesn't mean your life can't still feel manageable, familiar, or meaningful.

This exercise is here to help you **start redefining what normal looks like now—so you're not stuck chasing the past**, but building something you can actually live with today.

I give myself permission to...

...rest, even when everything isn't done.

Because *I'm exhausted and rest is part of how I survive this.*

I give myself permission to...

...feel sad that the life we used to have is gone.

Because *pretending I'm fine all the time isn't helping either of us.*

I give myself permission to...

...ask for help.

Because *I wasn't meant to carry this alone.*

Redefining Normal

Give yourself permission for something you need. Then, explain the reasoning behind why it's important to you right now.

Date _____

I give myself permission to... _____

_____

_____

_____

Because... _____

_____

_____

_____

Redefining normal doesn't mean choosing one new version of life and sticking to it forever. Your *"normal"* might look different week to week—or even day to day—and that's okay. What feels manageable today might feel impossible tomorrow, and what overwhelms you now might feel easier six months from now. **Give yourself permission to keep adjusting.**

Redefining Normal

Date

I give myself permission to...

Because...

---※---

Instead of searching for a big sense of normal, start by noticing the little things that feel steady—your morning routine, a quiet moment together, a task that now feels easier than it did a month ago. These moments can become anchors. Collect enough of them, and you might realize you're already living inside a new version of normal.

Redefining Normal

Letting go of the old version of normal doesn't mean forgetting what life used to be —it means making room for something new. You may already have small routines or quiet moments that feel steady, even if everything else still feels uncertain. Use this space to reflect on what your version of *"normal"* looks like right now, and how you might start to embrace it.

Date

Nothing ever goes back to normal. All that happens is your concept of normal changes.

-Allison van Diepen

Need more *Redefining Normal* pages?
Download free extras at: www.denisehoover.com/workbook

17

Letting Go of Who He Was

INSTRUCTION

Letting go of who your husband was before the stroke is a form of grief. You're not only mourning what happened—you're grieving the version of him you once knew. It's okay to miss that version; it doesn't mean you love who he is now any less.

But clinging to the past can make caregiving harder, bringing frustration and disappointment when things don't match the memory. Letting go isn't forgetting—it's making room for who he is today. It's about moving toward acceptance.

WHO HE WAS	WHO HE IS NOW
Great with money	Can't shop by himself
Loved being social	Sits quietly by himself
Planned our vacations	Gets overwhelmed with details
Could hold a conversation	Requires one subject at a time
Had a sense of humor	Takes jokes literally

What expectations are you still holding onto that may be causing pain or frustration?

What can you release today to make room for the version of him that's here now?

Letting Go of Who He Was

GUIDED ACTIVITY

Write your own *Then vs. Now* statements below. Think about the ways your husband has changed since the stroke—big or small. This isn't about judgment. **It's about gently noticing what's different, so you can start releasing old expectations and meeting him where he is today.**

WHO HE WAS	WHO HE IS NOW

Holding onto the *"before"* version of your husband adds to the emotional weight of caregiving. It can create distance, stir up resentment, or deepen the sense of loss you're already carrying.

Letting go of who he was isn't a betrayal—it's an act of love. It means making space for the version of him who exists today and giving yourself the freedom to connect in new ways.

Letting Go of Who He Was

GUIDED ACTIVITY

Letting go of who your husband was before the stroke doesn't mean forgetting or dismissing the man you married. It means honoring him while learning to embrace who he is now—with all his changes.

Complete the following *Letting Go* statements.
ex. I'm letting go of the guilt I feel for missing the man he was.

Date

I'm letting go of...

I'm letting go of...

I'm letting go of...

Letting Go of Who He Was

REFLECTION

One of the hardest parts of this journey is accepting that the man you once knew isn't coming back in the same way.

Use the space below to write a letter saying goodbye to who your husband used to be. Let yourself express any love, gratitude, or grief you're carrying.

Then, close your letter with one sentence that welcomes the man he is now into your heart and your life.

Date

 *Holding on is believing there is only a past; letting go is knowing there's a future.*
— Daphne Rose Kingma

Need more *Letting Go* pages?
Download free extras at: www.denisehoover.com/workbook

21

Calming Your Fear About the Future

Fear about the future is one of the heaviest parts of caregiving. It shows up in the quiet moments—those *"what if"* spirals that feel impossible to stop. You may worry about your husband's recovery, your own energy, your finances, or what happens if things get worse. That's normal. But fear grows stronger when you try to push it down.

You can't plan for everything, but you can ground yourself in what's true right now. **Naming your fear gives you back some control.**

What I'm afraid of...

I'm afraid my husband will never walk again.

What I know right now...

Right now, he's improving little by little, one step at a time.

What I'm afraid of...

I'm afraid my husband will have another stroke, and this time not make it.

What I know right now...

Right now, he's still here with me, and I need to enjoy my time with him.

You're allowed to acknowledge your fear without living in it.

Calming Your Fear About the Future

This page will help you get those thoughts out of your head and onto paper—where they can't control you anymore.

What I'm afraid of...

What I know right now...

What I'm afraid of...

What I know right now...

What I'm afraid of...

What I know right now...

Calming Your Fear About the Future

GUIDED ACTIVITY

Create an *Anchor List* that helps you stay calm when fear takes over.

Such as: Texting my sister, Taking three deep breaths, Sitting outside for five minutes, etc.

What helps me pause the fear and come back to the present moment?

When those *"what if"* thoughts start to take over, come back to this list.

Choose one thing that helps you feel grounded and bring yourself back to the present.

Calming Your Fear About the Future

REFLECTION

Fear about the future doesn't just disappear—but you can create a calming script to ground yourself when the thoughts become too loud.

Use this space to write a few words you can come back to when fear takes over. It might be something like, *"Yes, I'm afraid—but he's here right now. Focus on this moment."*

Let your words be honest, gentle, and something you'll believe when you need it most.

What I'm going to tell myself when the "what ifs" start getting loud:

Fear is always there; it's a survival instinct. You just need to know how to manage it.

— *Jimmy Chin*

Need more *Fear About the Future* pages?
Download free extras at: www.denisehoover.com/workbook

25

Planning

Organizing the chaos and reducing mental overload

Planning

Caregiving is overwhelming enough—you don't need your notes, appointments, and reminders scattered in a dozen different places.

In those first months, I remember trying to track medications, manage appointments, and explain my husband's condition to doctor after doctor, all while keeping our household afloat. It felt impossible—like juggling without hands.

Some days I sat at the kitchen table, buried in insurance papers and half-finished lists, with tears falling onto the pages. I wanted so badly to keep everything running smoothly at home while also being present for my husband's recovery. But there were times the bills went unpaid, chores piled up, and I felt like I was failing at it all.

Looking back, I wish I'd had a simple, central place to gather it all—a guide that would have made things feel more manageable and helped me feel like I had a little more control.

That's what this section is designed to be for you. A place to breathe, regroup, and sort through the chaos. These pages won't erase the stress, but they can give you a sense of order. Use them however you need—scribble all over them, print them out, or keep them blank until the moment is right.

Here, you'll find tools to help organize your daily, weekly, and monthly routines, prepare for medical visits, track medications and symptoms, and keep emergency information close at hand. There's even space to divide your life into categories so you can brain-dump the endless appointments, chores, and responsibilities that always seem to pile up.

Remember this isn't about doing it all or doing it perfectly. It's about finding a little structure in the middle of the storm. Take what helps, leave what doesn't, and give yourself credit for showing up, even on the hardest days.

When life feels overwhelming, planning is a way of telling yourself: "I've got this", one step at a time.

-Unknown

Essential Info

When everything feels like it's spinning, this is your one spot for everything that matters—the information you reach for again and again.

Use these pages to keep all the critical information—medical details, medications, emergency contacts, and documents—in one easy-to-access place.

Whether you're heading to an appointment, filling out forms, or facing an emergency, you won't have to dig. It's all right here.

MY HUSBAND'S INFO			
SOCIAL SECURITY #		DOB	
DATE OF STROKE			
DIAGNOSIS/CONDITIONS			
ALLERGIES			

INSURANCE	
PROVIDER	
MEMBER #	
GROUP #	
PHONE	

Essential Info

DOCTORS	
DOCTOR	
SPECIALTY	
ADDRESS	
PHONE	

DOCTOR	
SPECIALTY	
ADDRESS	
PHONE	

DOCTOR	
SPECIALTY	
ADDRESS	
PHONE	

Essential Info

HOSPITALS	
HOSPITAL	
ADDRESS	
PHONE	

HOSPITAL	
ADDRESS	
PHONE	

ELECTRONIC MEDICAL RECORDS	
WEBSITE	
USERNAME	
PASSWORD	

WEBSITE	
USERNAME	
PASSWORD	

Essential Info

MEDICATIONS			
MEDICATION NAME		START DATE	
DOSAGE		TIME(S) TO TAKE	
WHAT IT'S FOR			
PRESCRIBING DOCTOR			
NOTES/QUESTIONS			

MEDICATIONS			
MEDICATION NAME		START DATE	
DOSAGE		TIME(S) TO TAKE	
WHAT IT'S FOR			
PRESCRIBING DOCTOR			
NOTES/QUESTIONS			

MEDICATIONS			
MEDICATION NAME		START DATE	
DOSAGE		TIME(S) TO TAKE	
WHAT IT'S FOR			
PRESCRIBING DOCTOR			
NOTES/QUESTIONS			

Essential Info

MEDICATIONS			
MEDICATION NAME		START DATE	
DOSAGE		TIME(S) TO TAKE	
WHAT IT'S FOR			
PRESCRIBING DOCTOR			
NOTES/QUESTIONS			

MEDICATIONS			
MEDICATION NAME		START DATE	
DOSAGE		TIME(S) TO TAKE	
WHAT IT'S FOR			
PRESCRIBING DOCTOR			
NOTES/QUESTIONS			

MEDICATIONS			
MEDICATION NAME		START DATE	
DOSAGE		TIME(S) TO TAKE	
WHAT IT'S FOR			
PRESCRIBING DOCTOR			
NOTES/QUESTIONS			

Essential Info

DOCUMENTS		
	COMPLETED	LOCATION
DURABLE POWER OF ATTORNEY		
MEDICAL POWER OF ATTORNEY		
LIVING WILL/ADVANCE DIRECTIVE		
WILL		
TRUST		
LONG TERM CARE		
FUNERAL/BURIAL INSTRUCTIONS		

PASSWORDS		
WEBSITE	USERNAME	PASSWORD

Medical/Therapy Appointment Log

It's easy to forget what was said at appointments—especially when you're juggling so much.

Use these pages to jot down the important details: who you saw, why, what was discussed, and what's next.

Bring it with you to stay organized and ask the questions that matter most.

DATE		TIME	
PROVIDER		NEXT APPOINTMENT	
REASON FOR VISIT			
QUESTIONS TO ASK			
NOTES FROM VISIT			

DATE		TIME	
PROVIDER		NEXT APPOINTMENT	
REASON FOR VISIT			
QUESTIONS TO ASK			
NOTES FROM VISIT			

Medical/Therapy Appointment Log

DATE		TIME	
PROVIDER		NEXT APPOINTMENT	
REASON FOR VISIT			
QUESTIONS TO ASK			
NOTES FROM VISIT			

DATE		TIME	
PROVIDER		NEXT APPOINTMENT	
REASON FOR VISIT			
QUESTIONS TO ASK			
NOTES FROM VISIT			

DATE		TIME	
PROVIDER		NEXT APPOINTMENT	
REASON FOR VISIT			
QUESTIONS TO ASK			
NOTES FROM VISIT			

Medical/Therapy Appointment Log

DATE		TIME	
PROVIDER		NEXT APPOINTMENT	
REASON FOR VISIT			
QUESTIONS TO ASK			
NOTES FROM VISIT			

DATE		TIME	
PROVIDER		NEXT APPOINTMENT	
REASON FOR VISIT			
QUESTIONS TO ASK			
NOTES FROM VISIT			

DATE		TIME	
PROVIDER		NEXT APPOINTMENT	
REASON FOR VISIT			
QUESTIONS TO ASK			
NOTES FROM VISIT			

Need more Appointment Logs?
Download free extras at: www.denisehoover.com/workbook

Daily PLANNER

| S | M | T | W | T | F | S |

TODAY'S SCHEDULE

6 am	
7 am	
8 am	
9 am	
10 am	
11 am	
12 am	
1 pm	
2 pm	
3 pm	
4 pm	
5 pm	
6 pm	
7 pm	
8 pm	
9 pm	
10 pm	

SOMETHING FOR MYSELF TODAY
Even a small moment counts

TOP PRIORITIES FOR TODAY

☐ _____

☐ _____

☐ _____

☐ _____

WHAT I NOTICED TODAY

TODAY'S SMALL WINS

☐ _____

☐ _____

☐ _____

Daily PLANNER

DATE _____

| S | M | T | W | T | F | S |

TODAY'S SCHEDULE

6 am	
7 am	
8 am	
9 am	
10 am	
11 am	
12 am	
1 pm	
2 pm	
3 pm	
4 pm	
5 pm	
6 pm	
7 pm	
8 pm	
9 pm	
10 pm	

SOMETHING FOR MYSELF TODAY
Even a small moment counts

TOP PRIORITIES FOR TODAY

☐ _____

☐ _____

☐ _____

☐ _____

TODAY'S SMALL WINS

☐ _____

☐ _____

☐ _____

WHAT I NOTICED TODAY

Daily PLANNER

DATE _____

| S | M | T | W | T | F | S |

TODAY'S SCHEDULE

6 am	
7 am	
8 am	
9 am	
10 am	
11 am	
12 am	
1 pm	
2 pm	
3 pm	
4 pm	
5 pm	
6 pm	
7 pm	
8 pm	
9 pm	
10 pm	

SOMETHING FOR MYSELF TODAY
Even a small moment counts

TOP PRIORITIES FOR TODAY

☐ _____

☐ _____

☐ _____

☐ _____

WHAT I NOTICED TODAY

TODAY'S SMALL WINS

☐ _____

☐ _____

☐ _____

41

Daily PLANNER

DATE _____

| S | M | T | W | T | F | S |

TODAY'S SCHEDULE

6 am	
7 am	
8 am	
9 am	
10 am	
11 am	
12 am	
1 pm	
2 pm	
3 pm	
4 pm	
5 pm	
6 pm	
7 pm	
8 pm	
9 pm	
10 pm	

SOMETHING FOR MYSELF TODAY
Even a small moment counts

TOP PRIORITIES FOR TODAY

☐ _____

☐ _____

☐ _____

☐ _____

TODAY'S SMALL WINS

☐ _____

☐ _____

☐ _____

WHAT I NOTICED TODAY

Daily PLANNER

DATE _____

S	M	T	W	T	F	S

TODAY'S SCHEDULE

6 am	
7 am	
8 am	
9 am	
10 am	
11 am	
12 am	
1 pm	
2 pm	
3 pm	
4 pm	
5 pm	
6 pm	
7 pm	
8 pm	
9 pm	
10 pm	

SOMETHING FOR MYSELF TODAY
Even a small moment counts

TOP PRIORITIES FOR TODAY

- ☐ _____
- ☐ _____
- ☐ _____
- ☐ _____

TODAY'S SMALL WINS

- ☐ _____
- ☐ _____
- ☐ _____

WHAT I NOTICED TODAY

Daily PLANNER

DATE _____

S	M	T	W	T	F	S

TODAY'S SCHEDULE

6 am	
7 am	
8 am	
9 am	
10 am	
11 am	
12 am	
1 pm	
2 pm	
3 pm	
4 pm	
5 pm	
6 pm	
7 pm	
8 pm	
9 pm	
10 pm	

SOMETHING FOR MYSELF TODAY
Even a small moment counts

TOP PRIORITIES FOR TODAY

☐ _____

☐ _____

☐ _____

☐ _____

TODAY'S SMALL WINS

☐ _____

☐ _____

☐ _____

WHAT I NOTICED TODAY

Daily PLANNER

DATE _____

S	M	T	W	T	F	S

TODAY'S SCHEDULE

6 am	
7 am	
8 am	
9 am	
10 am	
11 am	
12 am	
1 pm	
2 pm	
3 pm	
4 pm	
5 pm	
6 pm	
7 pm	
8 pm	
9 pm	
10 pm	

SOMETHING FOR MYSELF TODAY
Even a small moment counts

TOP PRIORITIES FOR TODAY

☐ _____

☐ _____

☐ _____

☐ _____

TODAY'S SMALL WINS

☐ _____

☐ _____

☐ _____

WHAT I NOTICED TODAY

Need more Daily Planner pages?
Download free extras at: www.denisehoover.com/workbook

45

Weekly PLANNER

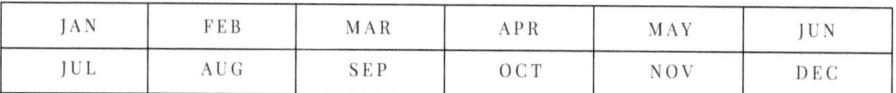

JAN	FEB	MAR	APR	MAY	JUN
JUL	AUG	SEP	OCT	NOV	DEC

MONDAY _____	TUESDAY _____	WEDNESDAY _____
_____	_____	_____
_____	_____	_____
_____	_____	_____
_____	_____	_____
_____	_____	_____

THURSDAY _____	FRIDAY _____	WEEKEND _____
_____	_____	
_____	_____	
_____	_____	
_____	_____	

THIS WEEK'S FOCUS

_____
_____
_____

LOOKING FORWARD

_____
_____
_____

Weekly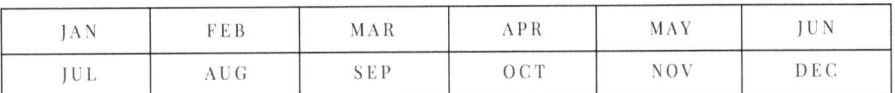

JAN	FEB	MAR	APR	MAY	JUN
JUL	AUG	SEP	OCT	NOV	DEC

MONDAY _____

_____

_____

_____

_____

_____

TUESDAY _____

_____

_____

_____

_____

_____

WEDNESDAY _____

_____

_____

_____

_____

_____

THURSDAY _____

_____

_____

_____

_____

FRIDAY _____

_____

_____

_____

_____

WEEKEND _____

THIS WEEK'S FOCUS

_____

_____

_____

LOOKING FORWARD

_____

_____

_____

Weekly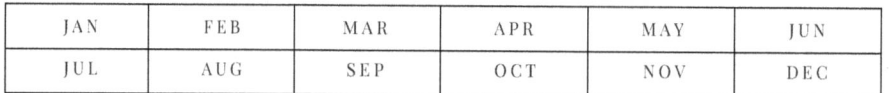

JAN	FEB	MAR	APR	MAY	JUN
JUL	AUG	SEP	OCT	NOV	DEC

MONDAY _____	TUESDAY _____	WEDNESDAY _____

THURSDAY _____	FRIDAY _____	WEEKEND _____

THIS WEEK'S FOCUS

LOOKING FORWARD

Weekly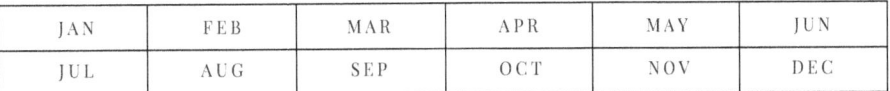

JAN	FEB	MAR	APR	MAY	JUN
JUL	AUG	SEP	OCT	NOV	DEC

MONDAY _____	TUESDAY _____	WEDNESDAY _____

THURSDAY _____	FRIDAY _____	WEEKEND _____

THIS WEEK'S FOCUS

LOOKING FORWARD

Monthly PLANNER

Year _____

JAN	FEB	MAR	APR	MAY	JUN
JUL	AUG	SEP	OCT	NOV	DEC

SUN	MON	TUE	WED	THU	FRI	SAT

THIS MONTH'S FOCUS

- ☐ _____
- ☐ _____
- ☐ _____
- ☐ _____
- ☐ _____

MUST DO TASKS

- ☐ _____
- ☐ _____
- ☐ _____

THOUGHTS AND REMINDERS

Monthly PLANNER

Year _____

JAN	FEB	MAR	APR	MAY	JUN
JUL	AUG	SEP	OCT	NOV	DEC

SUN	MON	TUE	WED	THU	FRI	SAT

THIS MONTH'S FOCUS

- ☐ _____
- ☐ _____
- ☐ _____
- ☐ _____
- ☐ _____

MUST DO TASKS

- ☐ _____
- ☐ _____
- ☐ _____

THOUGHTS AND REMINDERS

Monthly PLANNER

Year _____

JAN	FEB	MAR	APR	MAY	JUN
JUL	AUG	SEP	OCT	NOV	DEC

SUN	MON	TUE	WED	THU	FRI	SAT

THIS MONTH'S FOCUS

- ☐ _____
- ☐ _____
- ☐ _____
- ☐ _____
- ☐ _____

MUST DO TASKS

- ☐ _____
- ☐ _____
- ☐ _____

THOUGHTS AND REMINDERS

Monthly PLANNER

Year _____

JAN	FEB	MAR	APR	MAY	JUN
JUL	AUG	SEP	OCT	NOV	DEC

SUN	MON	TUE	WED	THU	FRI	SAT

THIS MONTH'S FOCUS

- ☐ _____
- ☐ _____
- ☐ _____
- ☐ _____
- ☐ _____

MUST DO TASKS

- ☐ _____
- ☐ _____
- ☐ _____

THOUGHTS AND REMINDERS

Monthly PLANNER

Year _____

JAN	FEB	MAR	APR	MAY	JUN
JUL	AUG	SEP	OCT	NOV	DEC

SUN	MON	TUE	WED	THU	FRI	SAT

THIS MONTH'S FOCUS

- ☐ _____
- ☐ _____
- ☐ _____
- ☐ _____
- ☐ _____

MUST DO TASKS

- ☐ _____
- ☐ _____
- ☐ _____

THOUGHTS AND REMINDERS

Monthly PLANNER

Year _____

JAN	FEB	MAR	APR	MAY	JUN
JUL	AUG	SEP	OCT	NOV	DEC

SUN	MON	TUE	WED	THU	FRI	SAT

THIS MONTH'S FOCUS

- ☐ _____
- ☐ _____
- ☐ _____
- ☐ _____
- ☐ _____

MUST DO TASKS

- ☐ _____
- ☐ _____
- ☐ _____

THOUGHTS AND REMINDERS

Balancing Life

It's hard to manage caregiving, home responsibilities, personal needs, and everything in between. You need a way to keep track of it all—break your life down into sections and list the things that need attention.

It's not about getting it all done—it's about getting it out of your head and onto the page.

PERSONAL

- ☐ *Schedule dentist appts*
- ☐ *Get birthday cards*
- ☐ *Christmas list*
- ☐
- ☐
- ☐
- ☐
- ☐

PROFESSIONAL

- ☐ *Research publishing*
- ☐ *Work on website*
- ☐ *Write Chapter 8*
- ☐
- ☐
- ☐
- ☐
- ☐

FINANCES

- ☐ *Call bank - Heloc*
- ☐ *Pay monthly bills*
- ☐ *Create Spreadsheet*
- ☐
- ☐
- ☐
- ☐
- ☐

SELF

- ☐ *Find yoga class*
- ☐ *Schedule nail appt*
- ☐ *Buy new journal*
- ☐
- ☐
- ☐
- ☐
- ☐

Balancing Life

Use the box below to do a brain dump. Write down everything that's weighing on your mind—big or small. The goal is to get it out of your head and onto paper.

This isn't a to-do list, and it's not about getting it all done. It's simply a way to declutter your mind and make space to breathe.

Balancing Life

Use the space on each page to label a specific area of your life that feels overwhelming. Then, group related items from your brain dump into that section.

When you're done, set this exercise aside for a couple of days. You've given yourself clarity—now you can come back to it one step at a time. The most important part was getting it out of your head.

_____

Balancing Life

Balancing Life

Balancing Life

—————— ❋ ——————

_____

Need more *Balancing Life* pages?
Download free extras at: www.denisehoover.com/workbook

61

Surviving

Reconnect with yourself and learn to embrace your evolving roles

Surviving

By the time my husband was a year into recovery, I felt completely drained. Exhaustion turned into resentment, and sometimes all I wanted was to escape. What I didn't realize at the time was that I was experiencing caregiver burnout—sometimes called caregiver syndrome. I had to find a way to keep showing up for my husband while also learning how to care for myself.

I realized I wasn't making space for the things that once brought me joy. I wasn't naming my emotions, let alone working through them. Journaling became the first tool that helped me pause and process. Putting pen to paper gave me permission to feel what I felt—and to see that I wasn't a bad person for having those feelings. I was simply human.

This section of the workbook is here to give you that same outlet: a place to process your emotions, name your wins and losses, and remember your husband's progress too. **These pages won't take away the pain or pressure, but they will help you release some of the weight you've been carrying.**

Here's what you'll find inside:

1. **Moments That Matter:** Space to record your husband's big and small improvements. I wish I had kept track of the small victories so I could remind him of how far he'd come when he felt stuck.
2. **Emotions From Within:** A journaling space with prompts to help you write freely. You can use these pages, or treat yourself to a beautiful journal and pen that make the process feel like self-care.
3. **Emotional Check-In:** A log to track your emotions over time. It will help you spot patterns, recognize triggers, and discover small ways to ground yourself when things feel overwhelming.
4. **If I Had a Day Off:** A creative exercise where you imagine a day away from caregiving. Whether it's something simple like a walk or something indulgent like a spa day. This is a chance to reconnect with yourself.
5. **Reframing Your Role:** Caregiving can stir up resentment. This activity helps you shift perspective, exploring who you were before and who you are now, so you can embrace your new role instead of fighting against it.

Surviving doesn't mean ignoring your feelings—it means finding ways to carry them without letting them crush you. My hope is that these activities help you reconnect with yourself, notice the small moments of progress, and feel less alone in the process.

Moments That Matter

Progress during stroke recovery can feel slow and uneven—some days move forward, others feel like a setback. But over time, even the smallest gains begin to add up.

Some signs of progress are loud—others are quiet and easy to miss. Use this space to notice and remember the little things: a new word spoken, a moment of independence, a flicker of humor, or a look of recognition.

These moments may seem small, but they're signs he's still in there—and he's still healing.

Date *July 2, 2023*

What he used to do/struggle with...

Jeff was struggling with recognizing the difference between a fork, knife, and spoon.

I often had to show him which one to use and how to hold it correctly.

What he did today...

Jeff started eating before I sat down with him. He didn't look to me for guidance or

ask which utensil to use. I stood in amazement, watching him eat his dinner.

Why this matters...

Progress!! My husband can eat by himself. It broke my heart to watch him struggle

with an ordinary, basic skill. Now, we can sit down and enjoy a meal together.

Make a point to notice and mention every bit of progress. Your husband may struggle to see it for himself.

Moments That Matter

Use these spaces to record a meaningful moments in your husband's recovery—
something he did, said, or understood that shows growth, no matter how small.

Date

What he used to do / struggle with...

What he did today...

Why this matters...

Date

What he used to do / struggle with...

What he did today...

Why this matters...

Moments That Matter

Date

What he used to do / struggle with...

What he did today...

Why this matters...

Date

What he used to do / struggle with...

What he did today...

Why this matters...

Moments That Matter

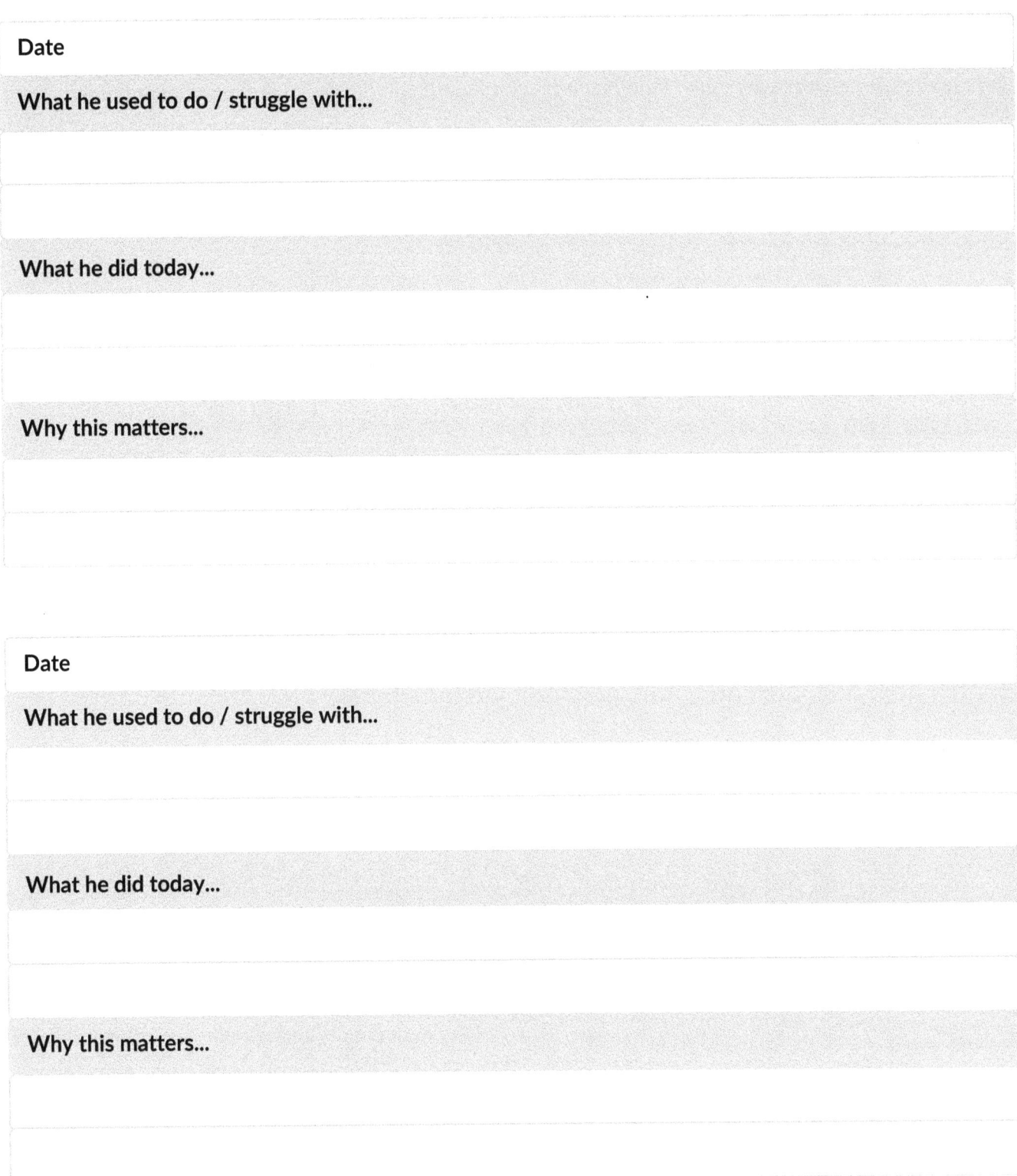

Date

What he used to do / struggle with...

What he did today...

Why this matters...

Date

What he used to do / struggle with...

What he did today...

Why this matters...

Need more *Moments That Matter* pages?
Download free extras at: www.denisehoover.com/workbook

69

Emotions From Within

Caregiving can leave your mind full and your emotions tangled. This space is for you—to write what you're feeling, question what you're thinking, or just breathe through the pen. **There's no right way to use these pages. Whether you're processing something painful or documenting something hopeful, let this be a release.**

Write it down. Let it out. Feel a little better.

What am I holding in that I wish I could say out loud?

Emotions From Within

Emotions From Within

What has been the hardest thing to accept during my husband's recovery?

Emotions From Within

Emotions From Within

What do I miss about the way things used to be?

_____

_____

_____

_____

_____

_____

_____

_____

_____

_____

_____

_____

_____

_____

Emotions From Within

Emotions From Within

What do I need, but haven't given myself permission to ask for?

Emotions From Within

Emotions From Within

How have I changed since becoming a caregiver?

Emotions From Within

Emotions From Within

What can I do for myself when I become overwhelmed?

Emotions From Within

Emotional Check-In

Caregiving comes with a constant swirl of emotions—some expected, others surprising. It's easy to get so caught up in daily responsibilities that you forget to check in with yourself.

This space is a simple way to pause and notice how you're really feeling.
There's no right or wrong answer—just honesty. Use it to name your emotions, recognize patterns, or get clarity when everything feels tangled.

Think of it as taking your emotional temperature. A small moment of awareness can go a long way.

Date _____

How am I feeling right now? (Check all that apply or add your own)

☐ Exhausted	☐ Lonely
☐ Numb	☐ Calm
☐ Hopeful	☐ Guilty
☐ Frustrated	☐ Determined
☐ Grateful	☐ Sad
☐ Angry	☐ Other _____
☐ Overwhelmed	☐ Other _____

Emotional Check-In

What's weighing on me today?

What do I need today—emotionally, physically, or mentally?
(e.g., rest, help, space, time outside, someone to talk to)

One small thing I can do for myself today...

Final thoughts or anything I want to let out:

Emotional Check-In

Date _____

How am I feeling right now? (Check all that apply or add your own)

☐ Exhausted

☐ Numb

☐ Hopeful

☐ Frustrated

☐ Grateful

☐ Angry

☐ Overwhelmed

☐ Lonely

☐ Calm

☐ Guilty

☐ Determined

☐ Sad

☐ Other _____

☐ Other _____

What's weighing on me today?

What do I need today—emotionally, physically, or mentally?
(e.g., rest, help, space, time outside, someone to talk to)

One small thing I can do for myself today...

Final thoughts or anything I want to let out:

Emotional Check-In

—— ✳ ——

Date _____

How am I feeling right now? (Check all that apply or add your own)

<table>
<tr><td>☐ Exhausted</td><td>☐ Lonely</td></tr>
<tr><td>☐ Numb</td><td>☐ Calm</td></tr>
<tr><td>☐ Hopeful</td><td>☐ Guilty</td></tr>
<tr><td>☐ Frustrated</td><td>☐ Determined</td></tr>
<tr><td>☐ Grateful</td><td>☐ Sad</td></tr>
<tr><td>☐ Angry</td><td>☐ Other _____</td></tr>
<tr><td>☐ Overwhelmed</td><td>☐ Other _____</td></tr>
</table>

What's weighing on me today?

What do I need today—emotionally, physically, or mentally?
(e.g., rest, help, space, time outside, someone to talk to)

One small thing I can do for myself today...

Final thoughts or anything I want to let out:

Emotional Check-In

—— ✳ ——

Date _____

How am I feeling right now? (Check all that apply or add your own)

☐ Exhausted	☐ Lonely
☐ Numb	☐ Calm
☐ Hopeful	☐ Guilty
☐ Frustrated	☐ Determined
☐ Grateful	☐ Sad
☐ Angry	☐ Other _____
☐ Overwhelmed	☐ Other _____

What's weighing on me today?

What do I need today—emotionally, physically, or mentally?
(e.g., rest, help, space, time outside, someone to talk to)

One small thing I can do for myself today...

Final thoughts or anything I want to let out:

If I Had a Day Off...

You give so much of yourself every single day. But what if, just for one day, the responsibilities were gone?

Use this page to imagine what a true day off would look like—for your body, your mind, and your spirit. No guilt, no restrictions. Just what you need.

Questions to explore:
- Where would I go?
- What would I wear?
- What would I do (or not do)?
- Who would I be with—or would I spend it alone?
- What would I eat, listen to, or watch?
- How would I want to feel?

Let your mind wander. Write freely. **This moment of imagination is a way to reconnect with yourself—and remember that you're still in there, too.**

If I Had a Day Off...

Reframing Your Role

You didn't choose this role—but here you are, doing your best every day. Still, caregiving can take over your identity if you let it.

This section helps you reframe how you see yourself—not just as a caregiver, but as a whole person navigating a complex situation.

You can still be a loving partner, a devoted spouse, and someone who values their own needs and voice.

Take a moment to look at this role from a different angle—one that allows room for both commitment and compassion (for yourself, too).

HOW I USED TO DEFINE MYSELF	HOW I DEFINE MYSELF NOW
Wife/Partner	*Nurse/Teacher*

Reframing Your Role

Step back from the *"I do everything"* identity and begin to view your role with more clarity, grace, and flexibility. It's not about denying the difficulty—it's about shifting perspective so it feels more sustainable and self-compassionate.

How has caregiving changed the way you see yourself—and how do you want that story to evolve?

Aphasia Exercises

Helping your husband communicate

Aphasia Exercises

Aphasia is one of the hardest parts of stroke recovery. It's not just about communication—it's about connection. When my husband struggled with aphasia, I saw how frustrating it was for him to know what he wanted to say but couldn't say it. It was hard for me too. Conversations that once came so easily suddenly disappeared. Some days it broke my heart. Other days it tested my patience. But still, we kept moving forward.

What I learned is that progress doesn't happen all at once. It comes in small, steady accomplishments: recognizing a letter, naming an object, writing a single word. These are victories. They may feel small in the moment, but together they form the baby steps that eventually lead to better communication—and hopefully, a conversation.

This section is not meant to replace speech therapy. These are simply tools and activities I used at home with my husband. They're designed to be simple, repeatable, and easy to use without special training. Think of them the way you would think of teaching a child to read: starting with the alphabet, learning sight words, recognizing everyday objects. Repetition matters. Patience matters. And celebrating the small wins matters most of all.

Inside, you'll find a handful of exercises—practical tools that gave us focus, practice, and even moments of laughter. You'll also find links to websites I used regularly for free resources, plus small tips to make daily life a little easier when aphasia is part of it.

In the beginning, your husband may struggle even with the simplest words or objects. Don't expect perfection. **What matters most is encouragement. Praise every attempt, no matter how small, and celebrate every success along the way.**

The goal here is not flawless speech. The goal is practice, progress, and making communication feel less frightening and more possible again.

Aphasia doesn't erase your husband's intelligence. It simply slows down the connection between his thoughts and his words. These exercises are a way to strengthen those connections, little by little, until you both start to see—and hear—progress.

Practice over perfection. Show up, try again, and let the small steps add up.

-Denise Hoover

Aphasia Toolkit

If your husband has aphasia, one of the most effective ways to support his recovery is to start simple—just like teaching an elementary student.

After a stroke, he may need to relearn the basics: the alphabet, everyday objects, common words, and how to put sentences together. This isn't about talking down to him—it's about meeting him where he is and helping him rebuild those language pathways with patience and encouragement.

The tools on this page are simple, affordable ways to practice at home, one small step at a time.

APHASIA "TOOLS"

- Word Search Books
- Notebook and Pen
- Elementary-level Flashcards (letters, words, pictures)
- Printed Worksheets (alphabet with sight words/money and making change)
- Dry-erase Board and Markers
- Storybooks with simple vocabulary
- Simple Board Games (like Memory or Go Fish)
- Sticky Notes
- Photos (recognizing familiar faces)
- Speech Therapy Videos
- Speech Therapy Apps
- Weekly Magnetic Write & Wipe Calendar
- Everyday Objects in your house
- Communication Boards (available for free online)

There's no set formula for recovery. Use your creativity to make these tools work for your husband in ways that fit your daily life. The following pages are examples to get you started.

Box of Everyday Things

Find a small box or container that can hold everyday household items.

Go room by room and choose 4–6 small objects to start with (examples are listed below). As your husband improves, you can increase the number to 8–10.

Give him a notebook and pen. One by one, have him take an object from the box and write down its name. When he's finished, hold up each object and ask him to say its name —without looking at what he wrote.

KITCHEN
Fork, Knife, Spoon
Cup
Spatula
Peeler
Sponge

BEDROOM
TV Remote
Eye Glasses
Candle
Book
Ear Buds

BATHROOM
Toothbrush
Dental Floss
Razor
Deodorant
Tweezers

OFFICE
Pencil
Envelope
Paper Clip
Scissors
Ruler

Box of Everyday Things

Praise every correct answer. If he struggles with an object, say the correct name and place the item back in the box to try again tomorrow.

Review his written list together, pointing out and helping with any misspellings.

Repeat this activity daily until he can name all the items correctly for several days in a row.

OTHER EVERYDAY ITEMS I WANT TO ADD LATER	

- Keep sessions short and positive—end on a win.

- Use items he would have easily known before his stroke.

- Use items that are meaningful to him.

- Celebrate small wins.

Paper Practice

————— ❋ —————

Worksheets may feel simple, but they can be powerful tools for rebuilding communication skills after a stroke. And many of them can be found online for free.

Just like teaching a child to read, these pages focus on repetition and familiarity—letters, sight words, numbers, and everyday objects.

The goal isn't to finish perfectly or quickly. The goal is to practice, repeat, and celebrate the small wins. Each word written, each letter recognized, and each problem solved is progress. Keep sessions short and encouraging.

Helpful Worksheets

Alphabet Tracing

Alphabet Chart

Sight Words

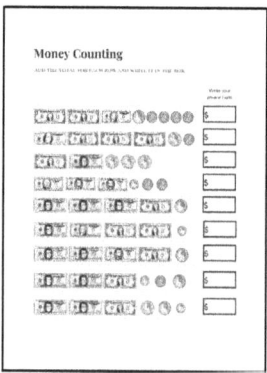

Money Counting

Making Change

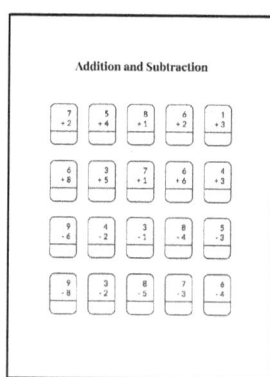

Simple Math

Paper Practice

There are many free resources available online to help your husband relearn and recognize words, objects, and everyday concepts.

Explore the websites listed below and choose the tools that best fit needs and current skill level.

This Reading Mama

thisreadingmama.com

- Free printable alphabet flashcards for letter recognition

- Tracing practice sheets

K5 Learning

k5learning.com

- Sight word flashcards

- Simple addition and subtraction worksheets

Super Teacher Worksheets

superteacherworksheets.com

- Printable coins and bills for practice

- Money recognition worksheets

- Giving change activities

Paper Practice

Super Star Worksheets

superstarworksheets.com

- Free printable worksheets

- Tracing practice sheets

Adult Speech Therapy Workbook

theadultspeechtherapyworkbook.com

- 75+ full-color naming cards

- Picture description activities

Bungalow Software

bungalowsoftware.com

- Custom communication board templates

- Step-by-step instructions to create your own

Helpful tips when using worksheets:

- Share one at a time so it doesn't feel overwhelming.

- Repeat familiar activities—they build confidence through repetition.

- Use plastic binder sheet covers and dry erase marker to make worksheets reusable.

Worksheet Instructions

Now that you've gathered your worksheets, the next step is learning how to guide your husband through them. It may feel intimidating at first, but it's actually simpler than it seems.

Think about helping a child achieve something they've never done before, You take it one small step at a time, giving clear, simple instructions and plenty of encouragement along the way.

The same approach works beautifully here. Stroke survivors often need directions that are slow, patient, and focused on one step at a time.

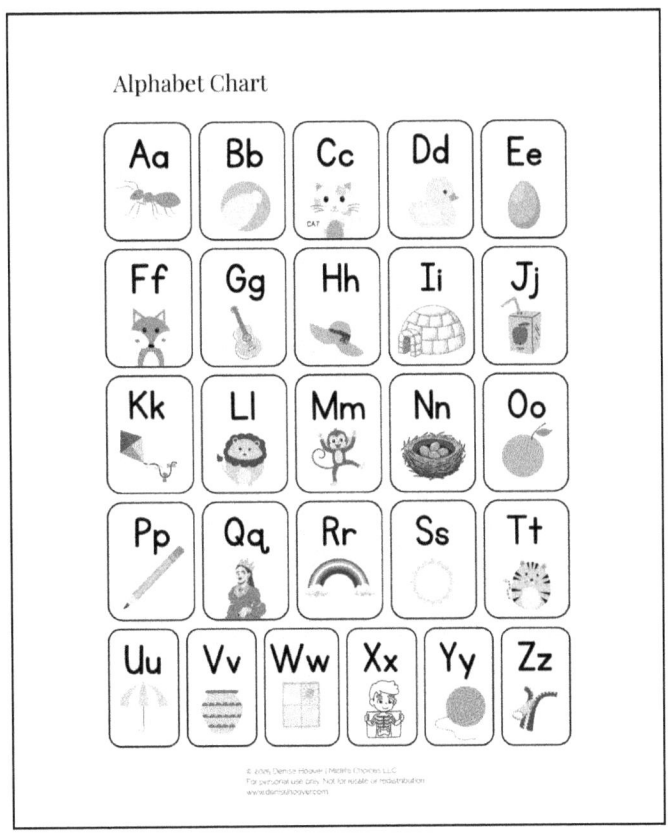

On the next pages, you'll find an example activity that shows how you can help your husband rebuild letter and word recognition using an Alphabet Chart—one small, encouraging step at a time.

Alphabet Chart

Worksheet

PURPOSE

Use this activity to help your husband reconnect letters with their names, sounds, and shapes. Start small—just a few letters at a time—and repeat daily.

INTRODUCE THE LETTERS

Point to each letter and say its name out loud. Ask your husband to repeat after you. Keep your tone calm and encouraging—this is about building comfort, not perfection.

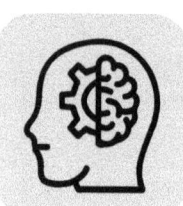

BUILD RECOGNITION

Once your husband feels comfortable with the letters, add the pictures that go with each one.

Example: "A: A is for Ant."

CONNECT TO EVERYDAY WORDS

Add meaning to the letters by connecting them to objects he knows.

Show a real apple or a picture of a word that starts with A.

Alphabet Chart

Worksheet

PRACTICE WRITING

If he's able to write, have him trace the letters while saying each one out loud.

When he's ready, move on to writing the words that match the pictures.

REPEAT AND ENCOURAGE

Repetition builds confidence. Go over the same few letters and pictures every day for several days before introducing new ones. Celebrate even small progress.

REFLECTION - CAREGIVER'S NOTES

Use the space below to jot down what letters he recognized easily, which ones were harder, and any progress you noticed from one day to the next.

Jeff recognized and wrote four letters today: A through D. He named six pictures,

but had a hard time with the word "guitar". I had him repeat it four times. We

will try to get more letters in tomorrow. He gets frustrated after 15 minutes.

Alphabet Chart

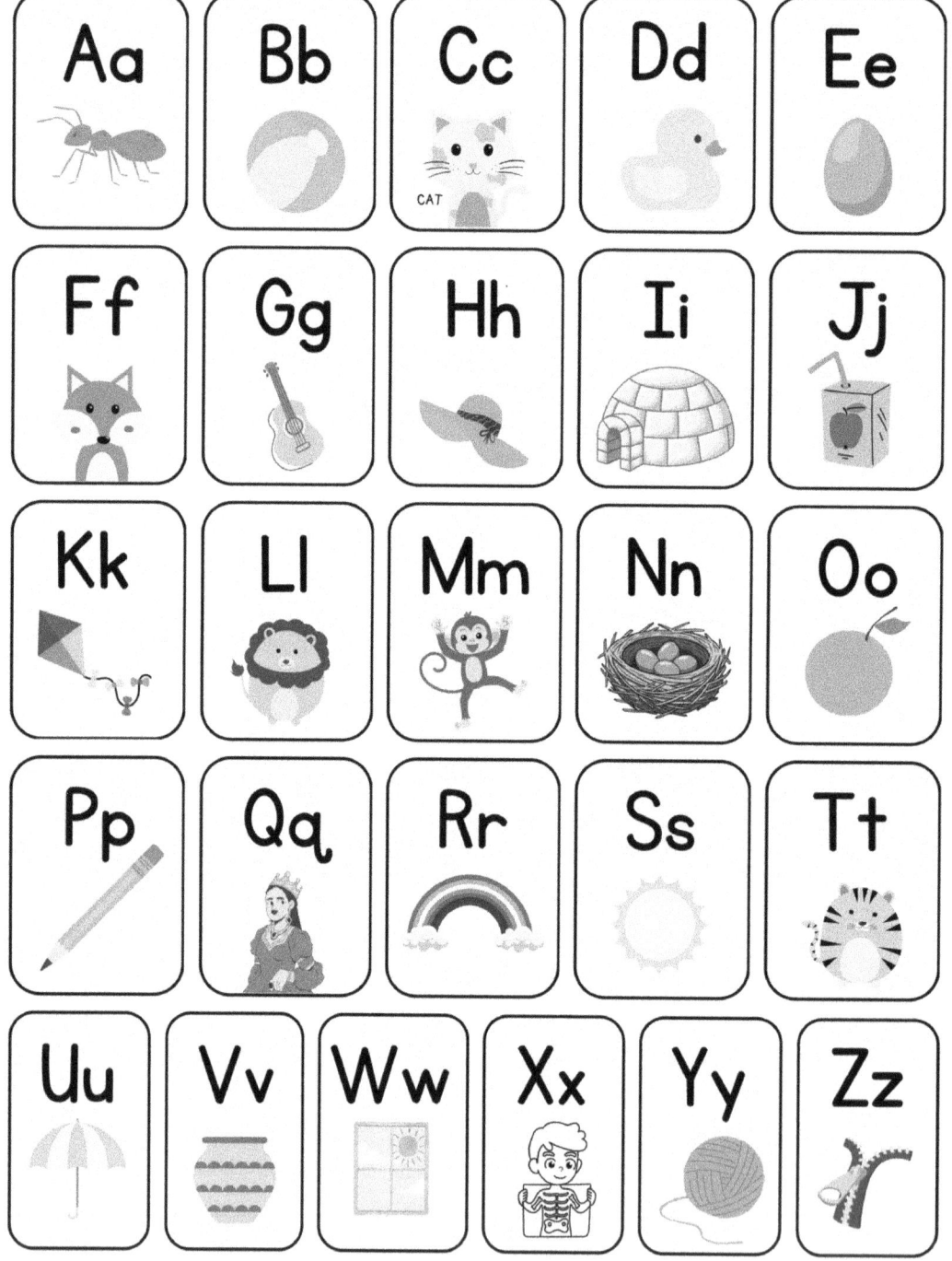

Worksheet Planner

Use this planner as a simple framework to walk your husband through any worksheet. Adjust the pace and steps as needed.

Worksheet

PURPOSE - What is the purpose of this worksheet?

INTRODUCE THE WORKSHEET - make it simple

RECOGNITION - build recognition through repetition

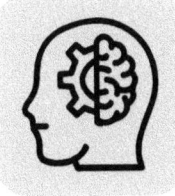

CONNECT TO EVERYDAY WORDS - show actual objects or pictures

PRACTICE WRITING - improvement comes through practice

REPEAT AND ENCOURAGE - repetition and praise are necessary

REFLECTION - CAREGIVER'S NOTES

Use the space below to jot down any progress you noticed from one day to the next.

Teaching Money

Learning to recognize and use money helps rebuild everyday independence.

Start with worksheets to identify coins and bills, then move to real money for sorting and counting. When he's ready, practice using money in real-life situations like paying for an item or making change.

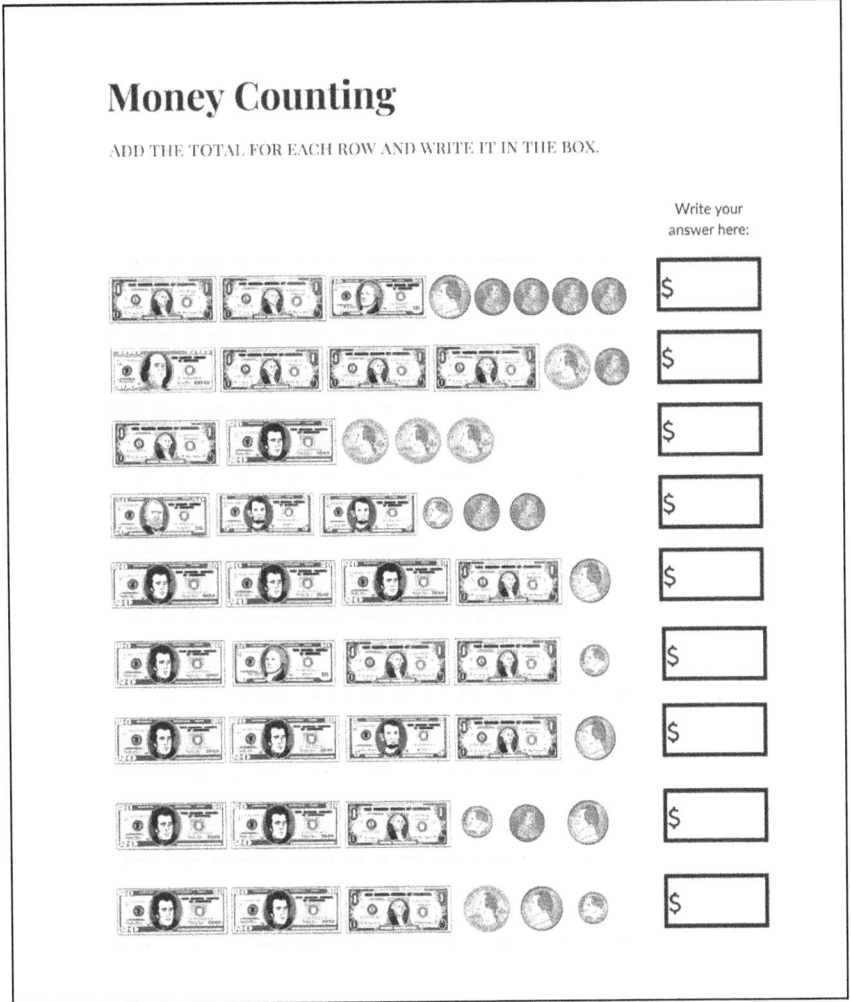

On the next page, you'll find specific instructions on how to teach and practice money recognition with your husband.

Teaching Money

PURPOSE

To help your husband relearn how to recognize coins and bills, count money, and make change—building confidence and independence one small step at a time.

MONEY RECOGNITION

Start with a simple worksheet showing coins and bills. Point to each one and name it out loud. Ask your husband to repeat the name and value.

Example: "This is a quarter. A quarter is worth twenty-five cents."

USING REAL MONEY

Once he recognizes coins and bills on paper, move to real money. Have him sort coins by type, count small amounts, or match bills to written prices.

Encourage hands-on practice—touching and handling the coins/bills helps memory.

REAL-LIFE PRACTICE

When he's ready, take the learning into everyday life. Role-play buying an item at home or let him pay for something small at a store.

Focus on the process, not perfection—each successful exchange builds confidence.

Money Counting

ADD THE TOTAL FOR EACH ROW AND WRITE IT IN THE BOX.

$

$

$

$

$

$

$

$

$

Everyday Appliance Practice

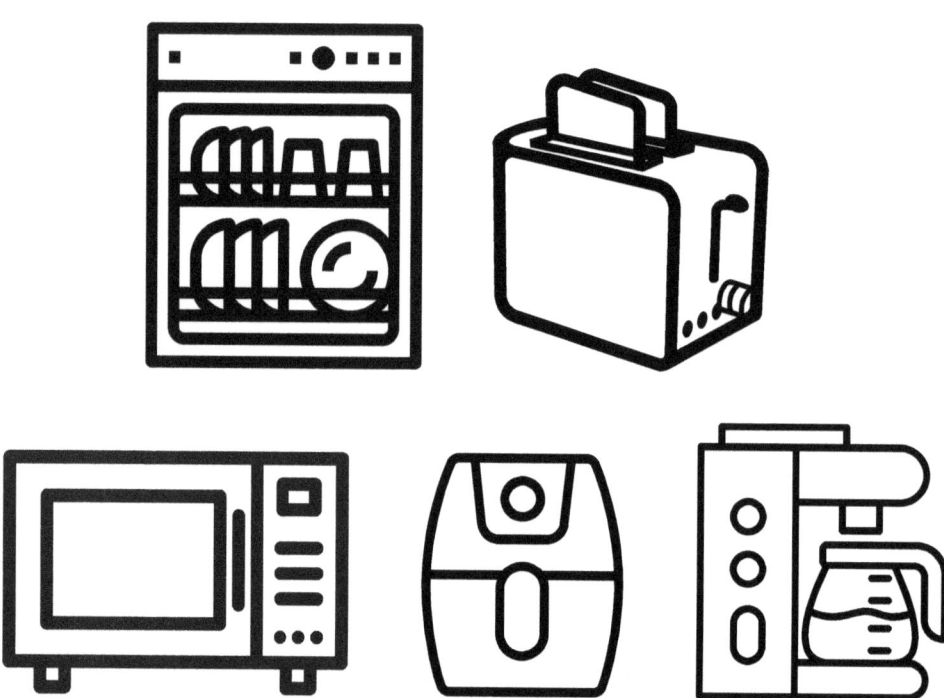

After a stroke, even familiar tasks—like using a coffee maker or air fryer—can suddenly feel confusing or unfamiliar. Your husband may not remember how to use the appliances he once operated daily, but that doesn't mean those skills are gone forever.

With a little help, patience, and repetition, confidence will start to return. This section walks you through simple, hands-on ways to help him relearn everyday kitchen tools safely—one button, one step, one small success at a time.

The example that follows focuses on using a toaster, since it's a common kitchen appliance and an easy one to start with. Every brand may look or function a little differently, but the way you teach remains the same—slow, step-by-step instruction.

Everyday Appliance Practice

Toaster

Appliance

INTRODUCE THE APPLIANCE

- Explain its use: *"The toaster warms and browns bread."*
- Show where the bread goes and how to lower the lever.
- Have him say or repeat the word toaster and name the parts.

DEMONSTRATE FIRST

- Plug in the toaster and toast a slice of bread while he watches.
- Narrate the process: *"We put the bread in. Then we press the lever down. When it pops up, it's ready."*
- Let him watch the bread pop up so he understands what happens.

GUIDED PRACTICE

- Have him place the bread in the slot and press the lever down.
- If he forgets, gently remind him step by step.
- Encourage him to describe what he's doing as he does it.

REINFORCE UNDERSTANDING

- After the bread pops up, review together: *"What did we do first? What happens next?"*
- Encourage him to use the toaster again the next day to reinforce memory.

REPEAT AND BUILD INDEPENDENCE

- Over time, have him prepare his own toast start to finish.
- Offer praise at each stage.
- Add variations — like using a bagel or adjusting the browning setting — once he's comfortable.

Everyday Appliance Practice

———— ❖ ————

_____
Appliance

1   **INTRODUCE THE APPLIANCE**

2   **DEMONSTRATE FIRST**

3   **GUIDED PRACTICE**

4   **REINFORCE UNDERSTANDING**

5   **REPEAT AND BUILD INDEPENDENCE**

Need more *Appliance Practice* worksheets?
Download free extras at: www.denisehoover.com/workbook

Quick Tips

Quick Tips for Daily
Communication & Practice

1. Write & Wipe Board on the Fridge
Put a small magnetic whiteboard (11 x 9) on your refrigerator. Write "Today is..." on the top. Have your husband write the day and date each morning. This helps with time orientation and builds a daily writing habit.

2. Write & Wipe Weekly Calendar on the Fridge
Place a magnetic write-and-wipe weekly calendar on your fridge. Every Monday, sit down together to talk about the week ahead and fill it in. This simple routine helps with time awareness and remembering upcoming plans.

3. Naming Categories
Ask your husband to name a set number of items in a category—for example, five fruits or four pieces of furniture. Start as a spoken activity to spark conversation, and once it's mastered, try it as a writing exercise. This builds both cognition and speech skills.

4. Tactus Therapy
Explore the Tactus Therapy app for speech exercises. It offers a variety of activities and tracks your husband's progress over time. Visit www.tactustherapy.com/aphasia to learn more.

You've made it through some of the hardest pages—and probably the hardest days. What you've written, faced, and worked through here matters.

Recovery continues, and so does your strength. Come back to these pages whenever you need to. Each time, you'll see your progress a little more clearly.

There's no finish line for this kind of healing. There's just showing up, caring, and doing your best—again and again. If you've made it this far, you've already done more than you realize, and your husband is lucky to have you.

Stay strong. You will survive.

Coming Soon ...

Midlife Choices

Are you a midlife woman feeling stuck in a rut, longing to rediscover your passions and unlock your full potential?

Filled with inspiring stories, practical guidance, and empowering exercises, this book will help you:

- Uncover your authentic desires and dreams
- Overcome limiting beliefs holding you back
- Develop a clear vision for your "second act"
- Take strategic action to turn your vision into reality

Whether you're seeking a career change, a new hobby, or simply a renewed sense of purpose, *Midlife Choices* will empower you to embrace the possibilities of this pivotal time in your life.

Rediscover your passion, reclaim your potential, and step into the thrilling unknown - the choice is yours.

Get updates at DeniseHoover.com